# Contents

**Unit**

# All About Me

*Your first writing is going to be about you, so that other people can get to know you.*

**Draw a picture** of yourself and your family.

Write the title Myself. Then write a **description** of yourself. It can be like this.

My name is _____. I am _____ years old.

I have _____ hair. (**what colour?**) I am _____ centimetres tall and I take size _____ shoes.

I live with my _____. (**mum? dad? who?**) My mum (or dad) gets cross with me when I _____ and is most pleased with me when I _____.

The clothes I most enjoy wearing at home are _____. (**describe them**) My favourite food is _____. My favourite toy is _____ and my favourite television programme is _____.

At school the lesson I like best is _____. The work I find hardest is _____. What I would like to be better at is _____. Outside school, what I most enjoy doing is _____.

Add anything else that you think is interesting about yourself.

Show this to your teacher or to other children in your class so that they can get to know you better.

**Remember**   Use a capital letter

to start every sentence.

for the names of people and pets (Lola, Snoopy, Mrs Ellis).

for the names of places (Bash Street, Liverpool, Africa).

# Weekends

Think about the sorts of things you do at weekends. What do you enjoy doing on Saturday mornings or on Sunday afternoons?

Make a chart like the one below:

| Things I like doing every weekend. | Things I enjoy occasionally. | Things I wish I didn't have to do. |
| --- | --- | --- |
|  |  |  |

Choose one activity from your chart. Where do you do it?
Who with? Describe exactly what happens.

**Extra Idea**

Make a concertina book about yourself.

When it's finished you could give it as a present.

# You Tell the Story

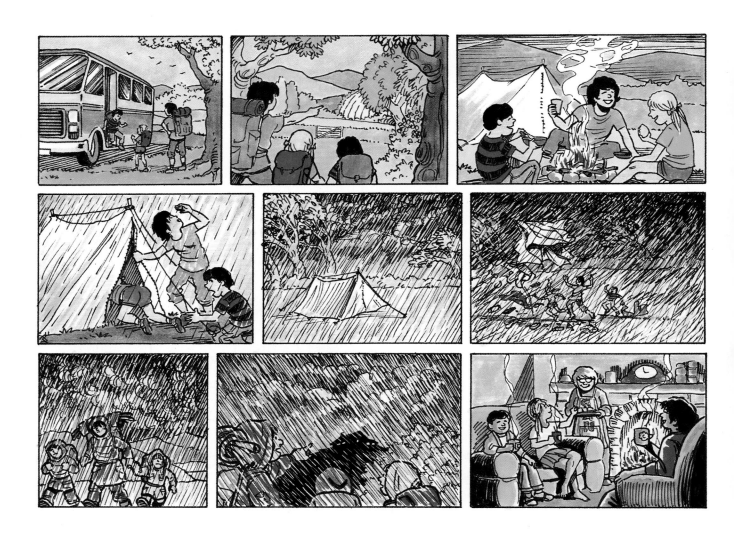

Tell this story in your own words, adding plenty of detail.

What did people **say**?

Describe the place where they camped. Why did they choose it?

How did they feel when the first raindrops fell? What did they say?

Describe the storm. How did they manage the tent?

Think of a good title.

4

Tell or write this story in your own words. This time **you** have to decide how the story ends.

You can work with a friend if you like.

# How a Famous Author Works

*Val Biro has written and illustrated at least thirty-five books. He also did the pictures for this book on pages 5, 18 and 19. He is best known for his stories about a vintage car called Gumdrop.*

We asked him about how he writes.

*How do you think of ideas and characters?*

**Val Biro**   Well, I started with my old car. I really do have an old car. I bought it ages ago and adored it. Then a publisher suggested I write a story about it.

I thought – what shall I call the car? I called it Gumdrop because when you switch on the ignition it goes Gu-u-u-um and then Drrrropopopop! And I invented a nice old man to own it and called him Mr Oldcastle.

*How do you make up new stories about Gumdrop?*

**Val Biro**   Often funny things *do* happen. Once Gumdrop's engine really did blow up! Then I thought I'd like to bring my dog into the story – so why not let the dog find a new engine? You can always change things to make them funnier.

Horace the dog is now Gumdrop's best friend – there's a story on page 5 to prove it. It is a constant worry to leave Gumdrop unattended, especially when there are vintage car thieves around! So Mr Oldcastle asked Horace to mount guard.

*Do you start with a picture or with writing?*

**Val Biro**   Sometimes a picture, sometimes a story.

*Do you make mistakes?*

**Val Biro**   Yes, I make false starts and have to begin again.

*Do you make draft copies?*

**Val Biro**   Yes, here's my first draft for 'Gumdrop's Merry Christmas'. It shows lots of corrections and how new ideas have to be fitted in.

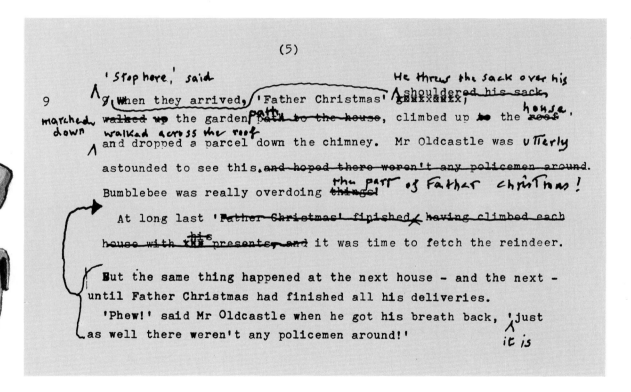

What gives **you** ideas for stories?

Do you prefer to start with a picture or writing?

Do you sometimes make false starts and need to begin again?

Would it help sometimes to make draft copies?

You can turn to pages 24, 31 and 43 for some suggestions for stories.

# Special People

Read this description of a little boy.

Does it make you feel you have really got to know him?

### My Nephew

My nephew is called Simon. He is one year old, but he is coming up to two. He has dark hair. I call him 'Vampire' because he keeps on biting people. He bit a friend on his hand till it started bleeding.

He likes hiding things like apples, pens, books. He has a little bike. He's like Barry Sheene. The second he's on it he can thump hard. He can also play Hide and Seek. You hide. He seeks. He can find you easily. He's a good runner too, when he's not tripping up over his toys. He's also a good climber. He climbs up the chairs and down, but sometimes he falls off. He has a little hiding place under the table. He's got a habit of leaning on chairs or tables with his hand in his pocket. He looks like an old man. He watches television. He likes The Dukes of Hazzard and The Muppet Show.

Once Simon stood on a little rock at Brimham Rocks. That day it was windy, so when Simon stood up the wind blew him down again.

Simon is very funny. Sometimes he's very lively too and, by the end of the day you're more exhausted than Simon. I like Simon a lot. He's a good little person to play with. I'm glad he lives with us really. But we can't stop him running about. So we will just have to be exhausted by the little terror.

*Gavin Teasdale (8)*

Can you describe somebody you know well, as carefully as this?
It could be one of your school friends, or somebody in your family.

First make some notes on:

what he or she **looks** like,

the sort of things he **does**,

the things he likes and dislikes,

how you feel about him.

Then write a full description of your special person. Use your rough notes to help you.

You can draw a picture to go with it.

### Making Draft Notes

You make draft notes to help you remember things.

They need not be in your best handwriting.

You can cross things out and alter them.

You don't need to write complete sentences.

---

### Extra Idea

Think of a very happy time that you spent with the person you described. Where were you? What did you do? What did you say to each other? Write it as a story. You can begin One day I_____.

# Remember Remember...

 Read this poem about Bonfire Night. It reminds us of some of the nice things that happen, but also of the dangers.

## Firework Night

The sky is filled with sparks and flames;
the children rush about,
their cries are hardly heard among
the din of bangers, jumping jacks and rockets.

Dogs howl and cats cry –
Frightened of the noise.
The sky is filled with cordite smoke.
The fire is burning high.
Flashes here and crackles there.
A rocket soars into the sky.

Among all this noise nobody hears
a small child sobbing in the shade,
a banger exploded in his hand
and only he can feel the pain.

*Eric Simpson*

Why don't dogs and cats like fireworks? What should we do to help them?

Do you know of any children who have been hurt by fireworks? What happened?

Think of some **sensible rules** to prevent accidents on Guy Fawkes night.

 **Make a poster** telling people about one of your rules.

First, **in draft**, write out the words you are going to use. Don't use too many words or people won't bother to read it.

Then copy it out in big clear letters with a picture which everybody will notice.

Pin up your poster where a lot of people will see it.

# Rules

**POOL RULES**
1. No pushing
2. No running
3. No ball games
4. No ducking
5. No back dives
6. No bombing

Think of the rules in a swimming pool.

Do you think they are important? Why?

What might happen if there were no rules at the swimming pool?

Think of **one** other public place, such as a zoo, supermarket, library, street or adventure playground. Are there any things you must or must not do there?

**Write** the name of the place. Then write a list of the things you must or must not do there.

Which do you think is the most important rule in your list? Why?

Write I think the most important rule is _____ because _____.

**Extra Idea**

Think how you would deal with people who break your rules. Write down how you would stop them.

11

# Strange Life Cycles

*A life cycle is the story of a creature's life – how it is born, has babies, lives and dies.*

## The life cycle of a frog

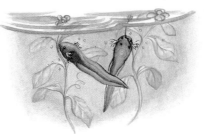

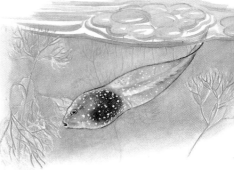

**1** The mother frog lays her eggs on the edge of a pond. The eggs are called spawn. Tiny tadpoles grow inside.

**2** The tadpole crawls out of its egg and holds on to a plant under the water.

**3** Then the tadpole swims off to find some food.

**4** The tadpole grows two back legs.

**5** Then it grows two front legs. Its tail grows shorter and it starts to poke its head out of the water.

**6** It crawls out of the water and hops away. After two years it will be the father or mother of more tadpoles.

What do you think a tadpole can find to eat in a pond?

Do you think it matters that the mother frog never sees her babies growing up?

How do you think a tadpole learns how to feed and look after itself?

Have you ever kept tadpoles in a jar? Did they grow up like the ones in these pictures?

# The life cycle of a duck

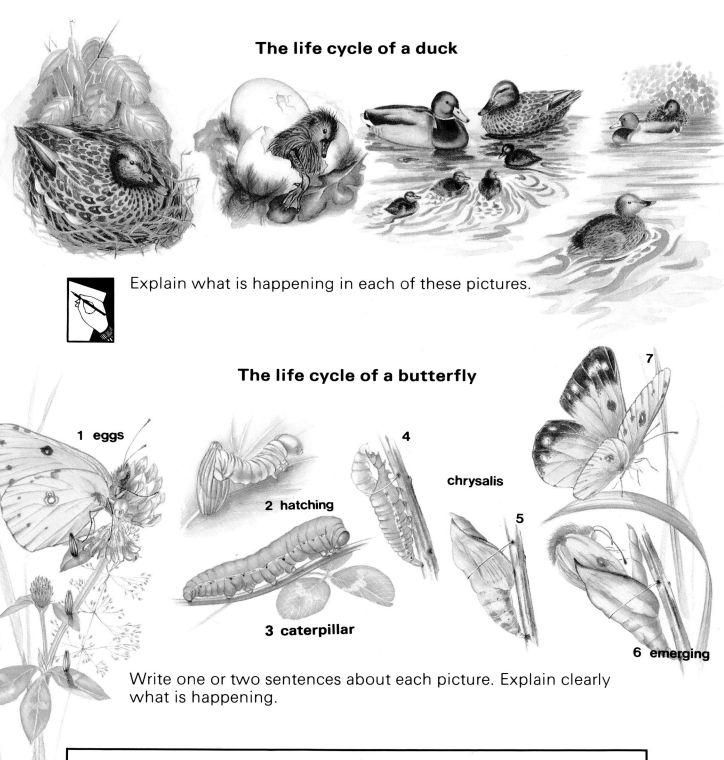

Explain what is happening in each of these pictures.

# The life cycle of a butterfly

1 eggs

2 hatching

3 caterpillar

4

chrysalis

5

6 emerging

7

Write one or two sentences about each picture. Explain clearly what is happening.

## Extra Idea

You might like to draw and write about the lives of more animals; for example, a fox, a hedgehog, a crocodile or a spider. You will need library books to help you.

# Explaining Things

*Are you good at explaining things?*

*Could you explain to somebody who has never done it before, exactly how to put on trousers or wash up?*

 Read these instructions. Something important has been left out. What is it?

**How to have a bath**

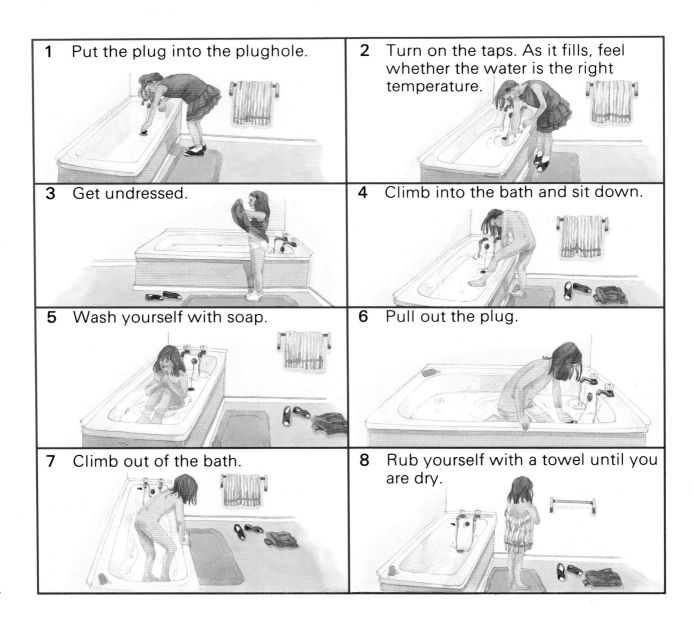

1   Put the plug into the plughole.

2   Turn on the taps. As it fills, feel whether the water is the right temperature.

3   Get undressed.

4   Climb into the bath and sit down.

5   Wash yourself with soap.

6   Pull out the plug.

7   Climb out of the bath.

8   Rub yourself with a towel until you are dry.

Look at these pictures showing how to use a telephone. Write out the five instructions to go with them.

## How to use a telephone

Now choose **one** of these to write. Make a rough copy first.

### How to wash your hair

Write the instructions which will go on the outside of the shampoo bottle.

### How to work your television set

Write out instructions for your friend. Tell her how to plug it in and switch it on and how to change the channels.

### How to make a sandwich

Write the instructions to go on the outside of a jar of peanut butter (or chocolate spread or marmite).

Or think of something else to write instructions for.

You can show your instructions to a friend to test them. He or she can pretend to carry out your instructions. Are they really clear? Did you miss anything out?

When you are sure that your instructions are correct write them out carefully.

# Amazing Stories

## The Cat in the Tree

There was once a girl called Rebecca who had a cat called Flame. One day Flame chased a squirrel up a tree. He climbed so high that he could not get down.

"Help!" shouted Rebecca. "My cat's stuck up in the tree!"

"Don't worry," said her dad. "I expect I can get him down." He got a ladder and went up the tree. But as he was reaching out for the cat, the ladder slipped down and he was left up in the tree.

"Help!" shouted Rebecca. "My cat and my dad are stuck up in the tree!"

"Don't worry," said her mum. "I expect I can get them down." She put the ladder up again and went up the tree. But, as she reached out for the cat, the ladder slipped and she too was left up in the tree.

"Who's going to help me now?" said Rebecca. "My cat and my dad and my mum are all stuck up in the tree!"

So Rebecca got an axe and chopped the tree down. Her mum and her dad and the cat all landed in a heap.

"Ouch!" said her mum.

"Ouch!" said her dad.

"Meeeow!" said the cat.

 Read again all the sentences which have **exclamation marks**.

What is special about them?

Exclamation marks are used when someone
shouts.
says something very funny.
says something very surprising.

Choose one of the picture stories below.

First, think of **names** for the characters.
Then, think of a **title** and write out the story.
Does anyone shout or say anything very surprising?

Or you can think of another amazing adventure to write a story about.

# Conversations

One way of telling a story is in a comic strip, like this:

Another way is to write it out as a play.

Two of you can read this out together. William must speak in a really scared voice. What sort of voice should Sonia use?

## A Funny Noise

Characters   Sonia
                 William

| | |
|---|---|
| <u>Sonia</u> | Did you hear a funny noise downstairs? |
| <u>William</u> | Yes. What do you think it is? |
| <u>Sonia</u> | I think it might be a burglar. |
| <u>William</u> | Oh no! What can we do? |
| <u>Sonia</u> | Of course it might be a ghost. |
| <u>William</u> | I'm scared of ghosts. I want my mum! |
| <u>Sonia</u> | Maybe it's a wild animal escaped from the zoo. |
| <u>William</u> | Ooh! I'm hiding! |
| <u>Sonia</u> | But it sounds a bit more like mum coming home. |
| <u>William</u> | Mum! |

Notice that we list the characters at the beginning. Every time someone speaks we start a new line. Then we underline the name and leave a space.

Now you write a play about two children who are left on their own. What will happen? Here are some ideas.

1  They see something strange through the window.

2  Water starts dripping through the ceiling.

# The Words People Say

In comics we put bubbles around the words people say like this:

In stories we put **speech marks** around the words people say like this:

"Look at this Dad! Quick!" shouted Moira.
"What is it?" asked her dad.
Moira showed him her strange contraption. "It's the first ever helicopter powered by fizzy lemonade," she said proudly.
"How does it work?" he asked.
Moira explained, "You shake the fuel tank hard like this . . . switch on the engine and . . ."
There was a loud explosion and Dad got soaked.

Speech marks are like comic bubbles. They go round people's words.

We put " when people start to speak.
We put " after the last word they say.

Now read this comic strip.

Decide on names for the characters. Then **write it out as a story**, using speech marks instead of bubbles.

You can begin: (name) and (name) crept up to the castle. The moon shone on its massive walls.
   "Look," whispered (name). "There's a light in that tower."

Carry on with the story. Does the rescue plan work or does it run into unexpected problems?

Think of a title.

# Spells

The witch on the left is called Gerty. The other two are warlocks (male witches). They are called Gussy and Goodge.

Gerty likes putting spells on children,

Gussy likes putting spells on grown-ups,

and Goodge likes putting spells on animals.

When they want to make a spell, they look in their *Horrible Spell Book*.

Here is one of Gerty's favourite spells:

Put into the cauldron:
2 bad eggs
3 fat frogs
a monkey's toenail.
Stir them up with vinegar and slimy greasy spider juice.

While you stir say:
Fatty frog
And monkey's toe
Make this child's nose
Grow and grow,
Then put a drop of the magic brew on the nose
of a little girl or boy.

What do you think this spell will **do** to people?

Here are some more pages from the *Horrible Spell Book*.

This is one of Gussy's spells:

Put into the cauldron
a bats tooth
2 tiger's stripes
and a squashed
banana
stir them up in
elephant's dribble
and octopus soup.

While you stir
say this spell...
Wobble Cobble
Catfish nobble
Make this man on
His knees to hobble.
Put the magic brew on
the feet of a man.

Put into the cauldron
a snake's eyelid
a wasp's wing
and a smelly kipper.
Stir them up with puddle
water and the juice
of a rotten cabbage.

While you stir
say this spell...
Eye of snake
Tongue of bat
Make this dog
sound like a cat.
Put a drop of the
magic brew on a dog.

This is one of Goodge's spells.

What do you think these spells will do?

Now make up your own spell.

Decide what it is going to do. **In draft**, make a list of funny things to put into your cauldron. Try to think of things that nobody else has thought of.

Now use the things on your list to make up a spell. It should be four lines long, but **it does not have to rhyme**.

Write it out beautifully on a big sheet of paper.

You can draw a picture of what happens when you put the spell on someone.

**Extra Idea**

Imagine you had magic powers for one day. What would you do? Describe what happens from the time you get up in the morning.

# Ideas for a Fairy Story

Here are some pictures to give you ideas for a fairy story. Choose **one** of them to write about.

Invent your own hero or heroine (the good person) and begin Once upon a time_____.

A magic bird comes out at night to steal things. Someone must catch it.

A cat can change into a lion when its owner says the magic word.

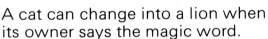

An old lady sells magic potions that can change people into different sorts of animals. Who buys her potions? What happens?

24

A goblin gives people magic apples. What happens?

A horrid wizard captures boys and girls and makes them work for him. Someone must rescue them.

A magic horse can help rescue people. But it behaves badly if the wrong person tries to ride it.

Two children get lost.

# Morning Sounds

Clink, clink, clinketty-clink –
The milkman's on his rounds, I think.
Crunch, crunch come the milkman's feet
Closer and closer along the street.
Then clink, clink, clinketty-clink –
He's left our bottles of milk to drink.

*Clive Sansom*

Do you sometimes hear the sound of the milkman early in the morning? What other sounds might you hear when you wake up?

Look at these pictures. Choose a word which goes with each one.

slamming

flushing

splashing

sizzling

clinking

chinking

banging

ringing

rattling

Do you think these words describe the sounds **exactly**?

Can you think of any other words to describe the sounds of frying sausages etc?

Invent some new words for some of the sounds. Would **whooshing** or **clunking** describe any of them?

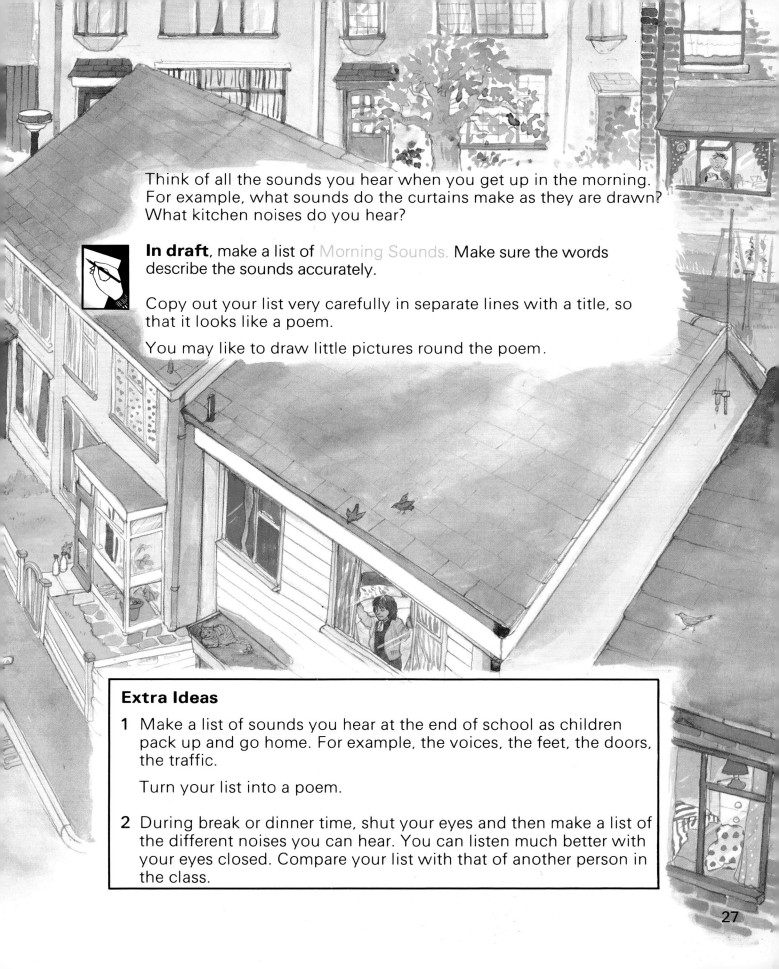

Think of all the sounds you hear when you get up in the morning. For example, what sounds do the curtains make as they are drawn? What kitchen noises do you hear?

**In draft**, make a list of Morning Sounds. Make sure the words describe the sounds accurately.

Copy out your list very carefully in separate lines with a title, so that it looks like a poem.

You may like to draw little pictures round the poem.

**Extra Ideas**

1 Make a list of sounds you hear at the end of school as children pack up and go home. For example, the voices, the feet, the doors, the traffic.

Turn your list into a poem.

2 During break or dinner time, shut your eyes and then make a list of the different noises you can hear. You can listen much better with your eyes closed. Compare your list with that of another person in the class.

# Hands that Touch

Little hurt bird
in my hand
your heart beats
like the pound of the sea
under the warmth
of your soft feathers.

*Charlotte Zolotow*

What does it feel like to touch something you like? This girl likes to touch her brother's curls:

I love to touch my brother's curls.
Everytime his hair is cut
I love running the curls across
 my hand
Twisting loosely in spirals
Never ending
So soft it never finishes.

*Susie (8)*

What does it feel like to touch something you hate? A boy called Daniel hates to touch raw meat. He wrote this poem:

Whose body has it come from?
It's all floppy and slimy.
It slithers in my hand.
It is so slippery.

*Daniel (8)*

Make a list of five things you like to touch. Then add five things you hate to touch.

Trace round the outside of your hands.

In the picture of your left hand, write the things you like. In the right hand, write the things you hate.

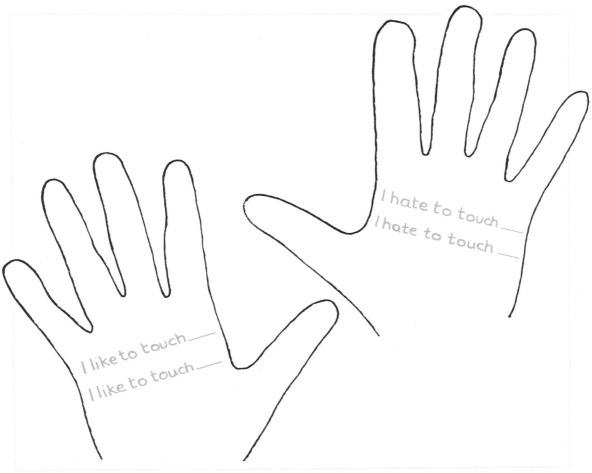

I hate to touch___
I hate to touch___

I like to touch___
I like to touch___

Choose one thing from your list of likes or hates and write about it. Make a draft copy first.

Think of words to describe what it really feels like. What do you think as you touch it? Does it remind you of anything?

Check over what you have written. Cross out or change any words you don't like.

Write it out carefully as a poem in short lines as Susie and Daniel did opposite. Then you can draw a picture to go with it.

29

# Making a Story More Interesting

Here is a very boring story:

**One day a girl went out in a boat. There was a big storm. She was shipwrecked on an island. She lived on her own until she was rescued.**

Why is it boring? How can we make it interesting?

What are the things we ought to **describe** or **explain**?

Now write your own version of the story.

Make sure you tell us:
— the child's name. It can be a boy or a girl or yourself.
— why she went out in the boat and what it was like.
— about the storm. What were the sea and sky like?
— how she was shipwrecked and how she felt.
— what she discovered on the island. Were there any strange creatures or plants?
— how she fed and looked after herself. Where did she sleep?
Tell us about any adventures or problems she had and how she was rescued. Try to make it really interesting.

Would any of these titles do?

Island in the Sun

My Terrible Holiday

The Creature on the Island

Can you think of a better title?

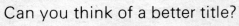

# Follow the Arrows

Start from the left.
Choose which arrows to follow.
You can work with a friend if you like.

It looked like an old ring.
(Describe it. What did you think
and say when you looked at it?
What happened? Was it magic?
Had it been stolen?)

we noticed something
strange on the ground.

It looked like a huge footprint.
(Describe it. What did you think
and say when you found it? Did you
discover whose footprint it was?
What happened?)

Or did you find something quite
different? Make up your own
story about it.

Start
here

One day I was
walking down
the road with
my friend
when . . . .

man riding a magnificent horse.
He was dressed all in green.
(Did he speak to you? Who was
he? What happened next?)

we met a strange
looking

woman carrying a heavy sack
on her back.
(Did she speak to you? Who
was she? Then what
happened?)

Or did you meet somebody else?
Make up your own story about
him or her.

# Things Falling

 Read this description of how a leaf fell from a tree.

When the leaf blew off the tree it swirled around in big circles. Sometimes it whooshed upwards and then circled around like an aeroplane deciding where to land.

Do you think this is an accurate description of rain falling?

When the raindrop fell it came straight down very fast. You couldn't see each drop until it landed and made a little splash.

A poet called James Kirkup wrote this description of snowflakes blowing in the wind.

They make no sound, they have no wings
and yet they can whirl and fly around
until they swoop like swallows, and
disappear into the ground.

Can you describe how something else falls? For example, how does a balloon fall? Or how does syrup fall as you drip it off a spoon?

Would any of these words help you?

zig-zag    drip    turn

flow    dribble

jump    flutter    ooze    glide    slide    drop    rush    tumble

Now carry out some experiments, watching how paper falls.

### 1st Experiment

1 Take a large sheet of paper (at least as big as this book).

2 Stand on a chair. Hold the paper out flat with both hands.

3 Let go of it. Watch carefully as it falls.

Did it fall straight down? Or did it change direction? Did it remind you of anything? **In draft**, write a sentence describing how it fell.

### 2nd Experiment

1 Take the same sheet of paper.

2 Stand on a chair. **Hold the paper by one corner** so that it hangs down.

3 Let go of it. Watch carefully as it falls.

Did it fall differently this time? **In draft**, write a sentence describing it.

If you want to compare them again, drop two sheets **together**, one flat, one hanging. See which reaches the floor first.

### 3rd Experiment

1 Crumple up the sheet into a ball.

2 Stand on a chair. Drop the paper.

Describe in rough how it fell **this** time.

## 4th Experiment

**1** Tear off a very small piece of paper, no bigger than this –

**2** Stand on a chair. Drop the piece of paper. Watch very carefully to see how it moves.

**3** Pick it up!

Describe in rough how it fell this time.

You have done four experiments. Like a scientist, you watched **exactly** what happened. The paper fell in a different way each time.

Now write a report like this, using your notes.

---

<u>Paper Dropping</u>

<u>Experiment 1</u>    We held the paper out flat and dropped it.
We saw that it _____
                    (Describe what you saw)

<u>Experiment 2</u>    We held the paper hanging down and dropped it.
We saw that it _____
                    (Describe what you saw)

<u>Experiment 3</u>    We crunched the paper into a ball and dropped it.
We saw that it _____
                    (Describe what you saw)

<u>Experiment 4</u>    We tore off a little bit of paper and dropped it.
We saw that it _____
                    (Describe what you saw)

The paper dropped **fastest** in Experiment _____ and **slowest** in Experiment _____.

---

Think about why the paper fell differently each time.

# Losing Things

Think of all the things that **you** have lost since you were little. Do you ever wonder what happened to them?

**Jackie writes:**

I was out with my mum at the shopping centre and she bought me a new pair of earrings. They were blue and sparkled. I put them on and felt grown up.

   We went to another shop to find school clothes. I was looking at them and I put my hand up to touch my earring.

   "Mum – my earrings! They've gone!" I shouted. I felt all weak and shaky.

   I looked and looked everywhere. I looked in all the clothes and on the carpets. We went back to every shop. Then my mum said, "Come on, we'll have to go home now. And cheer up. Somebody might find them for you."

   I was really sad. I expect somebody else is wearing them now. Every time I see a pair of blue earrings I think "I wish I could find mine". My mum says I can have another pair next Christmas but I might save up to buy some myself before then.

Can you remember a time when you lost something? If not, then imagine losing something very special.

What were you doing when you lost it? How did you know it was gone?

Where did you search?

How did you feel? What were you thinking?

What did your mum or dad say? (Remember the exact words)

How did it end?

Write a story describing what happened.

**Remember**   Questions always end with a question mark.

Where is it?      Have you seen them?

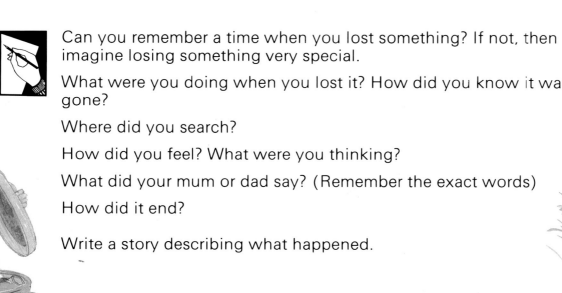

# Moods

Are you ever in moods like Kevin's or Gita's? Think of times when you felt like them.

## Kevin writes:

Sometimes I'm in a **creative** mood and I want to get on with building my moon buggy and nobody must touch it.

Sometimes I'm in my **wild** mood and I want to charge around being a space monster and jump out at people.

Sometimes I'm really **angry** and I feel it in my hands and toes and I feel like getting a grip on something and hurting it.

Sometimes I'm in a **lazy** mood and can't get out of bed and nobody must come near.

Sometimes I'm in a **helpful** mood and I help my mother sort out the shopping and put things away in the fridge.

**Gita writes:**

Sometimes I'm in a **nice** mood and want to be kind to people and everybody else seems nice too. And everything's right.

Sometimes I'm in an **excited** mood and just want to run around, like when I'm expecting Dad home after he's been away and Mum says I never stop talking.

Sometimes I'm in a really **horrid** mood, usually when I'm tired. I make mistakes and get cross. And somebody says "You've done it wrong" and I shout "I **don't** care!"

Sometimes Mum's been cross with me and I say I won't talk to her. But she always makes me talk by asking me millions of questions and I think I'd so like to answer her.

Sometimes I'm not cross or sad but **just sitting** there, having quite a pleasant time looking out of the window. I'm not caring about much, just daydreaming.

 Write the title Moods. Then write some sentences describing your different moods, as Kevin and Gita did. You can begin Sometimes I'm in a lazy mood. Then you can go on to your other moods.

# Being Brave

What frightened you when you were little?

Read this poem:

I felt afraid when I went on the ghost train.
I was four.
I felt afraid when a spider fell on me.
I was six.
I felt afraid when I went to somebody's house.
I was five.
I felt afraid when it was dark
   and the cars went bip bip.
I was eight.

*Kirsten (8)*

Now read this poem:

Bravery is
Getting up on a horse that looks like a mountain.
Opening my mouth wide at the dentist.
Telling my mum when I lost my gloves.
Knocking on Miss Johnston's door to tell her I had been fighting.
Taking horrible brown medicine.
Eating onions at my gran's.
Pretending not to be scared when I walk past the big Alsatian
   at the end of our street.

*Lisa (9)*

Which of these things do you think were the bravest?

Think of times when you have had to be brave. Write a poem like Kirsten's or Lisa's. Draw some little pictures to go around the poem.

---

**Extra Idea**

Describe a time when you had to be brave. Ask yourself how did it start? Who were you with? What was frightening about it? How did you feel? Draw a picture of it.

---

# Feeling Angry

 What do you feel like when you are angry?

Here are some children's answers:

When I am angry I could scream as loud as if the earth was blowing up. My face goes red hot. I make funny faces behind people.

*Neal (8)*

When I am angry I slam all the doors and I stamp my feet. I get sent to my room and I feel sorry and begin to cry.

*Emma (7)*

When I am angry I boil up inside. I go red then blue. My face goes very stern. I feel that I could blow up and murder the person who made me mad. I slam the door and stamp my feet and think "I'll kill him".

*Matthew (8)*

When I'm angry at my mother I feel all steamed up. When I go upstairs I stamp and try to get noticed. I want everybody to know I am cross. In my room I think of what to say when she comes in. I think of horrible words. But when she comes in she cheers me up.

*Charlotte (8)*

 What are you like when you are angry? Do you go red in the face or clench your fists?

How do you feel inside? Do you feel hot or cold? Do you want to hit something or someone?

Now write about Feeling Angry as the children above have done.

# Would You Buy It?

Look at this shop.

Why are some things half price?

How do shops try to persuade you to buy their goods?

Why do they want you to buy more things?

1 Write the title The Present I'd Choose. Think what you'd like to have from this shop if you had a gift token. **Describe** what you have chosen and **explain** why you want it.

2 Write the title A Present for Somebody. Choose something in the shop that you'd like to give to somebody. **Describe** it and **explain** why you think he or she would like it.

3 Think of something else that the shop **hasn't** got that it ought to have. **Write a letter** to the manager and say **why** the shop ought to sell it.

# Animal Stories

Tell or write this story in your own words. You can start One evening I went for a walk through the woods with my Dad.

Make sure you tell us how you **felt** and what you and your dad **said** to each other.

What did you say?

Now what did you say?

Why were you upset?

What did you see next morning?

What was your plan?

What did your parents say?

How did you look after it?

9 months later.

What did your parents say?

How did you feel?

Think of a good title for this story.

What do you think of the father's behaviour? Why do you think that?

Did the child do the right thing?

Choose one of these to write about.

## 1   The Mysterious Egg

One day I was walking near the river when I saw a huge egg _____.

What did you think?

What did you do?

What did people say?

What hatched out of it? Then what happened?

## 2 The Kitten in the Snow

Did mum allow the children to keep it?

Maybe later the kitten's real owner came in search of it. What did the child think and say then?

## 3 Escaped

A dangerous animal has escaped from the circus. How did you help to find it?

# What do People Really Say?

Would this girl say

or

> You can not catch me!
>
> You can't catch me!

Would this boy say

or

> What's for tea?
>
> What is for tea?

Would this lady say

or

> I will see you later
>
> I'll see you later

Would this man say

or

> You're not funny
>
> You are not funny!

Would this boy say

or

> It's not fair!
>
> It is not fair!

Look at the apostrophes ('). Can you explain why they are used?

## Apostrophes

Put an apostrophe where you miss out letters.

When people are talking:

**is not** changes to **isn't**    **do not** changes to **don't**
**it is** changes to **it's**    **I will** changes to **I'll**
**I am** changes to **I'm**    **let us** changes to **let's**

What do people say instead of these?

| | |
|---|---|
| that is | I would not |
| he is | he could not |
| we are | you must not |
| you have | we should not |

Can you think of any more shortened forms?

**Copy out** this opening for a story. Change the pink words into the shortened form using an apostrophe.

## The Incredible Invention

"**What is** that horrible object **you have** got there?" said my dad.
"Oh nothing, Dad," I said. "**It is** just something **I am** inventing."
"**You are** not bringing it into this house. Get it out!" he said firmly.
"Oh Dad!" I cried. "You **will not** even notice it once **it is** in my bedroom."

Check that you have put the apostrophes in the right places, then carry on with the story. What is the incredible invention you have been making? What does it do? What does your dad think of it?

# How People Talk!

Which people do you think are speaking very correct English?
We call this **Standard English**.

Which are talking in a friendly style, not bothering to be very correct?
We call this **non-standard English**. Can you think of other
examples of non-standard English that you often hear?

Read this passage about a Yorkshire boy who loves animals.

A boy was sitting under a tree playing on a rough wooden pipe. And on the trunk of the tree, a brown squirrel was clinging and watching him. From behind a bush a pheasant was stretching its neck and nearby there were two rabbits sitting up and sniffing.

He held up his hand when he saw Mary approaching.

"Don't tha move," he said. "It'd flight 'em. A body 'as to move gentle an' speak low when wild things is about."

*(From* The Secret Garden *by Frances Hodgson Burnett)*

 Notice that the **story** is written in Standard English, but the boy **talks** in non-standard English. Can you understand him? What is he saying?

Write a story **either** set in your playground at school, where something unusual might have happened, **or** about a child who could tame wild animals.

Include plenty of conversation – some of which might not be in Standard English!

# All Sorts of Stories

Look at these books.

Which are the witch and ghost stories? Which are the fairy stories? Which are the true-to-life stories? Which are the animal stories?

Which kind of stories do you most like to read? Which kind of stories do you most like to write? What sort of things happen in them?

Now do a **survey** to find out what other children think.

1 Copy out this chart.

2 Ask each child *What kind of stories do you like best?*

3 Put a tick for each answer in the appropriate column.

| Ghost | Fairy | True-to-life | Animal |
| --- | --- | --- | --- |
| | | | |

Now count up the number of ticks in each column. Make a graph of the results like this:

Ghost     Fairy     True-to-life     Animal

Ask people **why** they prefer one kind of story. Under the graph you can write a **report** like this:

The most popular stories are _____.

People like them because _____.

The second most popular are _____.

People like them because _____.

**Extra Idea**

You can make a survey of older and younger children in your school. Do they like different sorts of stories?

# Have You Read any Good Books?

 Think of any story books that you have read or listened to lately. Did you enjoy them? Would other children like them?

Write a **review** of a book so that other people will know what it is like. This is how you can do it:

A review of _____ by _____
        (name of book?)        (author?)

I _____ a book called _____.
  (read? listened to?)

I _____ I thought it was _____.
(enjoyed it very much? quite        (exciting? sad? funny?
enjoyed it? did not like it?)       mysterious? scary? what else?)

The character I liked most was called _____ who was a _____.

One of the best things that happened was _____.

I found it _____ to understand.
          (quite easy? a bit difficult?
          very difficult?)

The sort of people who would enjoy this book are _____
aged _____ to _____.
                        (boys? girls?
                        boys and girls?)

Make a wall display of book reviews to help other people choose books.

# A Book You Should Read

 Look at these posters. Do they make you want to read the books?

 Draw a poster advertising a book which you think people should read.

First make a draft copy. Write the name of the book in big letters in the middle of the page. Add the author's name in small letters.
Then draw a rough pencil sketch of something happening in the story.

In the space that is left, write one or two exciting sentences which will make people want to read it. Check the spelling!

Copy it out carefully on a big sheet of paper. Make it colourful.
Perhaps you can pin it up in the book corner or library.

# Characters to Write about

These characters have already appeared in books which you can find in the library. Decide which of them you want to write about.

Later you might like to read the original book to see whether it is like your story.

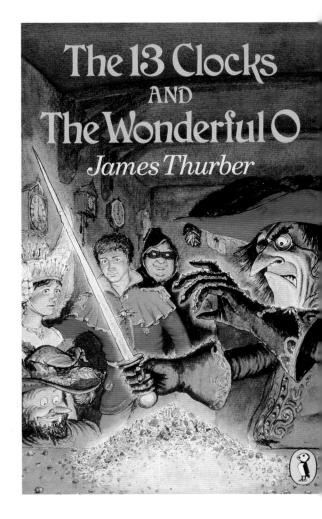

Once upon a time, in a gloomy castle on a lonely hill, there lived a cold cruel Duke. His nights were spent in evil dreams, and his days were given to wicked schemes . . .

Does he try to do something specially wicked? Does somebody get captured in his castle? Who wins in the end? Invent a really good story about him.

## Conversation

Remember to have plenty of conversation to make your story interesting.

Keep asking yourself: How does the character *feel?*

What would he or she *say?*

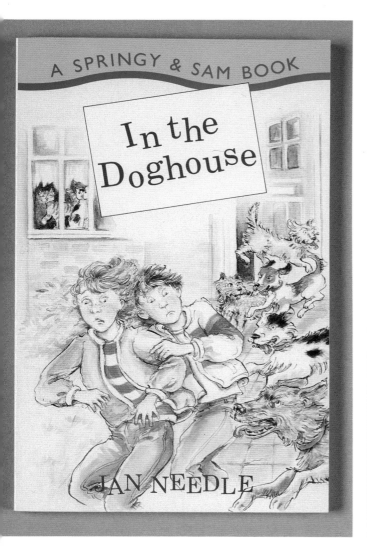

A SPRINGY & SAM BOOK

In the Doghouse

JAN NEEDLE

ASTRID LINDGREN

PIPPI

Longstocking

Springy (a boy) and Sam (a girl) are twins. Sometimes they fight, but usually they are friends.

They have to do a project for their teacher about something *unusual*. They do it about a mysterious, deserted old house. They explore it and discover some very strange things going on there.

Imagine you have a twin and you explore an empty house together. What happens?

Pippi was a very remarkable child, and the most remarkable thing about her was her strength. She was so strong that in all the world there was no policeman as strong as she. She could have lifted a whole horse if she had wanted to. And there were times when she did want to.

Think what sort of things Pippi does.

Write a story about her.

# Letters

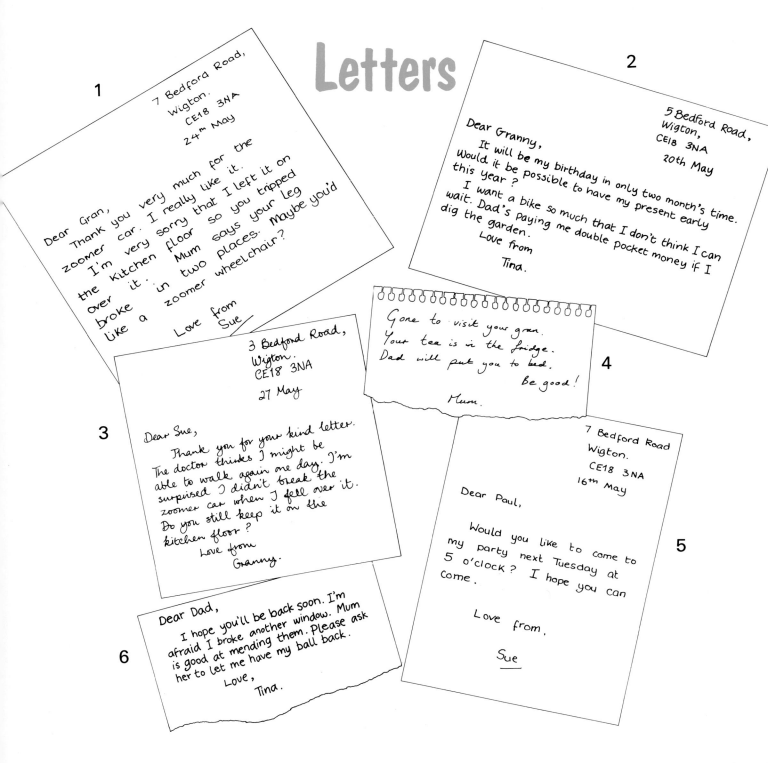

**1**

7 Bedford Road,
Wigton.
CE18 3NA
24ᵗʰ May

Dear Gran,
Thank you very much for the zoomer car. I really like it. I'm very sorry that I left it on the kitchen floor so you tripped over it. Mum says your leg broke in two places. Maybe you'd like a zoomer wheelchair?
Love from
Sue

**2**

5 Bedford Road,
Wigton,
CE18 3NA
20th May

Dear Granny,
It will be my birthday in only two month's time. Would it be possible to have my present early this year?
I want a bike so much that I don't think I can wait. Dad's paying me double pocket money if I dig the garden.
Love from
Tina.

**3**

3 Bedford Road,
Wigton.
CE18 3NA
27 May

Dear Sue,
Thank you for your kind letter. The doctor thinks I might be able to walk again one day. I'm surprised I didn't break the zoomer car when I fell over it. Do you still keep it on the kitchen floor?
Love from
Granny.

**4**

Gone to visit your gran.
Your tea is in the fridge.
Dad will put you to bed.
Be good!
Mum.

**5**

7 Bedford Road
Wigton.
CE18 3NA
16ᵗʰ May

Dear Paul,
Would you like to come to my party next Tuesday at 5 o'clock? I hope you can come.
Love from,
Sue

**6**

Dear Dad,
I hope you'll be back soon. I'm afraid I broke another window. Mum is good at mending them. Please ask her to let me have my ball back.
Love,
Tina.

 Read these letters. Then look at the picture opposite and decide who wrote each letter.

Why do you think 4 and 6 don't have addresses?

 Did you work out who wrote the letters?

Now write some **replies**:

1 from **Gran** explaining why she can't afford to buy Tina a bike and she'll be getting a nice doll instead;

2 from **Paul** explaining why he can (or cannot) come to Sue's party;

3 from **Tina's dad** saying he is very cross about the window and she will have to pay for it.

**Remember**   Lay out your letter correctly.

---

**Extra Idea**

**Write a real letter** that you can send or give to someone. It could be:

a thank you letter for a present or for something nice that has happened;

a letter to your teacher asking her to organize a special class visit, and explaining where you want to go and why it is a good idea;

a letter telling somebody some news about yourself.

Remember to put your address and the date at the top.

# Dreams

On a Saturday afternoon in the football season
I lie in a bed near the lake
And dream of moles with golden wings.

*Robert Bly*

Read this boy's poem about a horrible dream:

I dream that –
I am being chased by a creature.
It has a great nose
Like a beak.
It gets bigger and smaller.
It's poison and I must run.
I am running everywhere.
I run to next door to get away.
Their door slams,
The great nose is caught in the door
But still chasing me.
I am running, running.
I climb a tree,
Then I'm safe.

*Paul (9)*

## Long Live the Queen

I went to bed quite late, ten o'clock I think. I went up the stairs slowly. Soon I reached the bedroom door.

When I got into the room I knelt down to get into the bed. I wrapped the covers over. When I closed my eyes I saw a palace covered in gold, and there I was sitting on a throne. There was a long table. It had chickens and wines and puddings on it. People were eating and making merry. There I was, servants were offering me drink and food. I felt so important.

People looked at me and said, "Long live the Queen". I smiled at them contentedly. Then suddenly I saw a black picture, as dark as the night.

I woke up expecting to see servants around me. But all I saw was my same old room, with the same old wall.

I closed my eyes trying so hard to see the beautiful dream, but I didn't.

*Gillian McAnuff (11)*

Do you ever dream? Do you have nice or nasty dreams?

Try to remember some of your dreams. Do you sometimes move very slowly? Do you meet any strange creatures?

Now write about your dreams. If you cannot remember any of your dreams, then make one up.

You can write a poem, as these children have done. Draw pictures, as a border, round what you have written.

# Cat Cat Go Away

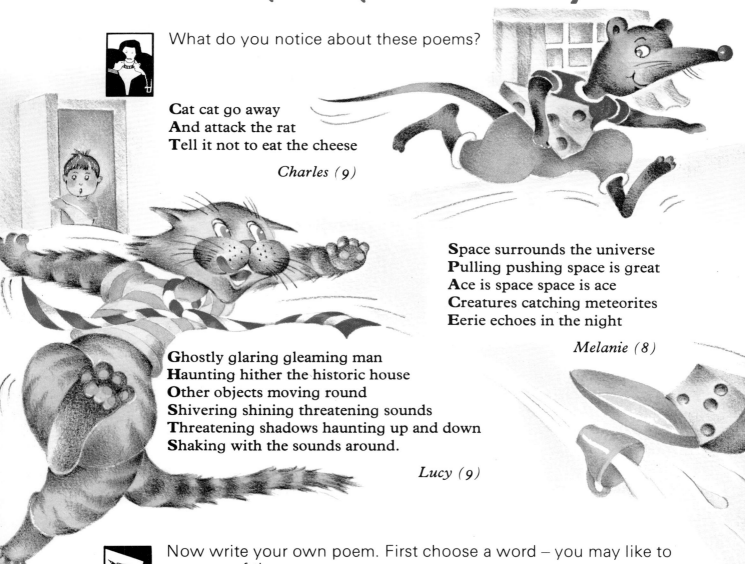

What do you notice about these poems?

**C**at cat go away
**A**nd attack the rat
**T**ell it not to eat the cheese

*Charles (9)*

**S**pace surrounds the universe
**P**ulling pushing space is great
**A**ce is space space is ace
**C**reatures catching meteorites
**E**erie echoes in the night

*Melanie (8)*

**G**hostly glaring gleaming man
**H**aunting hither the historic house
**O**ther objects moving round
**S**hivering shining threatening sounds
**T**hreatening shadows haunting up and down
**S**haking with the sounds around.

*Lucy (9)*

Now write your own poem. First choose a word – you may like to
use one of these:

LIONS        SISTER

DRAGON     ICE CREAM

BATS         SUMMER

In rough, write the letters of your word down the side of the page, then
write your poem. Each line should say something about the thing you are
writing about, but it doesn't have to rhyme.

When you are happy with it, copy it out. Colour the first letter of each line
so that it stands out.

# I Know Someone

## I Know Someone

I know someone who can
take a mouthful of custard and blow it
down their nose.

I know someone who can
make their ears wiggle.

I know someone who can
shake their cheeks so it sounds
like ducks quacking.

I know someone who can
throw peanuts in the air and catch them
in their mouth.

I know someone who can
balance a pile of 12 2p pieces on his elbow
and snatch his elbow from under them
and catch them.

I know someone who can
bend her thumb back to touch her wrist.

I know someone who can
crack his nose.

I know someone who can
say the alphabet backwards.

I know someone who can put their hands in
their armpits and blow raspberries.

I know someone who can
wiggle her little toe.

I know someone who can
lick the bottom of her chin.

I know someone who can
slide their top lip one way
and their bottom lip the other way

and that someone is
ME.

*Mike Rosen*

Do you know people who can do funny things? Write a poem like
the one above, starting I know someone who can _____ (You
can *pretend* to know some funny people if you like.)

# Secret Places

Read this description by a boy called John Conway.

## Building a Den

I built a great den. First I got some wood. There was a lot of wood and I brought a barrel. I made the sides first then the roof with the barrel. I got my pals. We nailed it all up then we put sheets of metal on so that no one could harm the wood. It was rocket shaped with a screen inside it and cardboard buttons on it. We played at taking the rocket to other planets and pretended that there were monsters outside.

Have you ever had a secret place where you can hide?

Imagine you have a perfect secret place. Would it be far away from grown-ups? Would you let your friends go there? Or would you play there alone?

Describe your secret place in detail.
Where is it? (It could be in a real place.)
What is it made of? How did you build it?
What does it look like?
What is it like to be inside?

## Extra Idea

Imagine that something exciting happened in your secret place. Maybe there was a great storm? Or perhaps you were hiding in it when you noticed some suspicious characters nearby. Write a story about it.

# Other Ideas for Writing

Think of a TV programme you watch regularly. **Write a review** of it so that somebody who has never seen it will know what sort of things happen in it, and what are the good and bad things about it.

Imagine that it's **raining** again! What do children in your school do when they can't go outside at break time? Think of some good ideas for games and activities to keep everybody happy and out of mischief. **Write out some instructions** called 'What to do in wet playtimes.'

Is there any special outing or activity which you wish your teacher would organise for your class? Think of something really interesting and **write a letter** trying to persuade your teacher to do it. You must explain clearly *why* you want it to happen and what it would be like.

**Write a horrible story or play** to scare your teacher and give the other children bad dreams. Imagine that all the dogs (or cats or mice or birds) mysteriously started to grow bigger and bigger and bigger so that they were as big as houses and ran round wild.

Write the title **Reasons for Writing**. Make a list of all the reasons why you write (to do sums or to sign your pictures, for example). Then write about what sorts of writing you find hard and what you find easy; and in what ways you could make your writing better. What was the best piece of writing you have done this year? What was good about it?

**Write a poem** about growing up. Some of the lines can begin:

When I'm bigger I'll . . .

*Or* write a poem about a monster. Some lines can begin:

Look at its . . .

# Pictures for You to Write About